Cornerstones of Freedom

The Story of

The Battle of Chancellorsville

Zachary Kent

CHILDRENS PRESS®

CHICAGO

Library of Congress Cataloging-in-Publication Data

Kent, Zachary.
    The Battle of Chancellorsville / by Zachary Kent.
    p. cm. – (Cornerstones of Freedom)
    ISBN 0-516-06679-X
    1. Chancellorsville (Va.), Battle of, 1863 – Juvenile literature.
[1. Chancellorsville (Va.), Battle of, 1863. 2. United States –
History – Civil War, 1861-1865 – Campaigns.]
I. Title. II. Series.
E475.35.K46 1994
973.7'34 – dc20   94-9486
                                                      CIP
                                                      AC

In the mid-1800s, a bitter argument raged in the United States over slavery and states' rights. The country was torn in two. In the South, cotton was the major crop. It was grown on large plantations worked by African slaves. Southerners depended on slavery for the success of their farming economy. Most northerners considered slavery cruel and immoral. The northern economy was based on factory production, and these factories employed thousands of European immigrants.

Abraham Lincoln

The election of Abraham Lincoln as United States president in 1860 brought the conflict over slavery to a head. Angry southerners feared

Southern cotton farmers used black slaves to work their fields.

An 1861 map shows the eleven southern states that seceded from the Union.

Jefferson Davis

that Lincoln, a northerner from Illinois, would abolish slavery. They insisted that the federal government had no right to force laws upon the individual states. Rather than submit, eleven southern states decided to leave the Union. They formed the Confederate States of America, with Jefferson Davis as their president.

In April 1861, Confederate cannons bombarded Fort Sumter in the harbor of Charleston, South Carolina, forcing the withdrawal of the Union garrison. The Civil War had begun.

President Lincoln called for volunteers to put down the South's rebellion. He vowed to hold the United States together at all costs. The land soon shook with the crack of musketfire and the crash of thundering cannons. Some of the

4

hardest fighting occurred on Virginia battlefields. In battle after battle, the fierce Confederates turned back Union advances on the Confederate capital of Richmond.

Fifty-six-year-old General Robert E. Lee commanded the Confederate Army of Northern Virginia. At the Battle of Fredericksburg, Virginia, in December 1862, Lee's spirited soldiers held a strong defensive position and slaughtered rows of attacking Yankees, who were under the command of Ambrose E. Burnside. The battered Union army lost more than 12,000 men at Fredericksburg; the surviving soldiers limped to winter camps north of the icy Rappahannock River.

Robert E. Lee

The South fires on Fort Sumter — the battle that launched the Civil War.

The Union Army at Fredericksburg, Virginia

After the disaster at Fredericksburg, President Lincoln searched for a new commander to take over the Union Army of the Potomac, which was fighting the Confederates in Virginia. In January 1863, Lincoln gave the command to Major General Joseph Hooker. Lincoln told Hooker, "Go forward, and give us victories."

Northern newspapers had nicknamed Hooker "Fighting Joe" because of his proven bravery in battle. Hooker hated the nickname, however, because he thought it portrayed him as hot-headed and too eager to fight.

Hooker spent the late winter months plotting his plan of attack on General Lee. Fresh troops

and supplies arrived from the North. By the
spring of 1863, Hooker had 132,000 men under
his command, a unit that Hooker claimed was
"the finest army on the planet." He further
bragged of his strategy for the spring battle:
"My plans are perfect, and when I start to carry
them out, may God have mercy on General Lee,
for I will have none."

   With the two armies still facing each other
near Fredericksburg, Hooker planned to leave
about 40,000 Union troops there under the
command of Major General John Sedgwick.
While Sedgwick occupied Lee at Fredericksburg,
Hooker would take the rest of his forces
northwest along the Rappahannock River, loop
southeast, and attack Lee from the rear. Lee's

62,000 men would be crushed between Hooker and Sedgwick's forces.

At first, everything went according to Hooker's plan. On April 27, 1863, three Union corps began tramping twenty miles up the Rappahannock. Two days later, Hooker's blue column of soldiers turned southeast and marched through a dense forest known as The Wilderness. The Yankees soon reached a clearing where five roads came together, ten miles west of Fredericksburg. A red-brick, white-columned mansion stood there called Chancellor House. The Chancellor family kept a farm and ran their house as an inn. As a result, the country

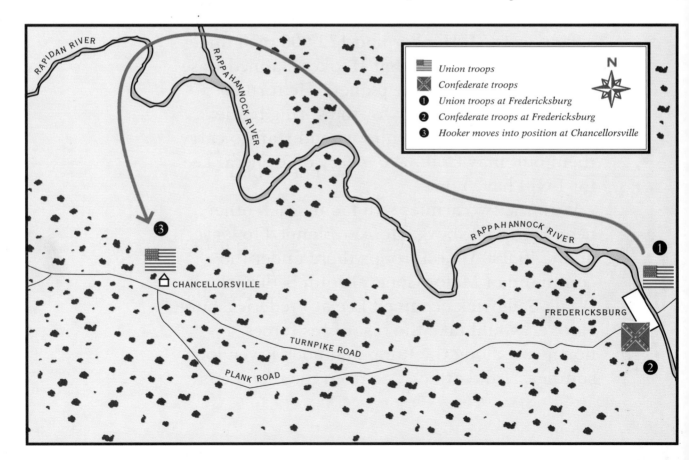

After completing his flanking move, Hooker set up Union headquarters at the Chancellor House.

crossroads was called Chancellorsville. As his troops were assembling at the Chancellorsville crossroads, Hooker and his generals were pleased — they had successfully moved very close to Lee's flank without Lee knowing it.

But by April 30, scouts had indeed informed General Lee of Hooker's troop movements. Lee later explained that he was well aware that "the main attack would be made upon our flank and rear."

Lee's response was a bold strategic risk, one that went against all military teaching. Even though he was surrounded by two tremendous Union units, he decided to split his troops in

Thomas "Stonewall" Jackson was Robert E. Lee's leader in the field.

two. He left Jubal Early's division of just 10,000 men to guard Fredericksburg against 40,000 Union troops sitting across the river. Meanwhile, Lee's remaining 40,000 troops hurried westward to meet Hooker's 70,000 Yankees at Chancellorsville.

Thirty-nine-year-old Lieutenant General Thomas J. "Stonewall" Jackson led the Confederate march toward Chancellorsville. Jackson had won the nickname "Stonewall" for holding his ground at the First Battle of Bull Run in 1861. Jackson's continued battlefield successes in 1862 had made him a hero throughout the South.

On May 1, 1863, Hooker put his attack plan in action. He advanced his Union army eastward, expecting to surprise Lee from behind at Fredericksburg. But after only two miles, the sudden roar of Confederate artillery halted the Yankee march. Stonewall Jackson was attacking, throwing the Yankees off balance.

Cannonshells exploded in the thick woods. Rebel soldiers fired rifles from behind the trees. Hooker was caught completely by surprise. Hooker ordered an immediate retreat to Chancellorsville. Even his own officers could not figure out why Hooker would retreat when he had reached the moment to attack. Rumors later persisted that he had been drinking, but many of his officers denied that charge. In the end, Hooker admitted that he had simply lost confidence in himself.

Back at Chancellorsville, Hooker ordered his bewildered troops to dig in for defensive

Fighting breaks out in the dense woods of The Wilderness.

*Jackson proposes
his bold strategy
to Lee in their
midnight meeting.*

positions. They spent the night chopping down trees and digging trenches. They built a long defense line facing east and south.

Late that night, Lee and Jackson met in the forest along the Confederate battleline near an ironworks called Catherine Furnace. Warming their hands over a fire, they discussed their options. Rebel cavalry officers had reported that the west end of the Union defense line was hanging "in the air," open and unprotected. Lee saw an opportunity to strike where the Yankees would least expect. He gave Jackson the task of planning the attack.

"What do you propose to do?" asked Lee.

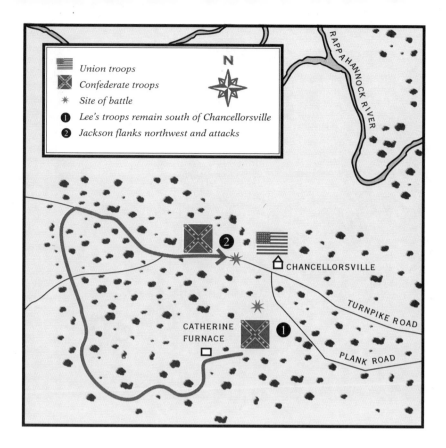

Jackson pointed to a map and ran his finger along a backwoods route that led west. "Go around here," he said.

"What do you propose to make this movement with?" asked Lee.

"With my whole corps," said Jackson.

Jackson's daring proposal meant moving 26,000 troops close across the front of the entire Union army. The plan would spread the entire Confederate army dangerously thin, splitting it into three small portions: Jackson's 26,000 marching in a long, narrow column; Lee's 14,000, who would have to hold the attention of Hooker's main force at Chancellorsville; and

Jackson's corps creeps quietly through the woods, trying not to be noticed by Union scouts.

Jubal Early's 10,000, still staring down the 40,000 Yankees at Fredericksburg.

Despite the high risk in the plan, Lee trusted Jackson entirely and approved his strategy.

With grim urgency, Jackson ordered his infantry to begin its march, telling them to move quickly and quietly. A local citizen guided the Confederates through the thick woods along a hidden wagon trail. The string of marching, silent Rebels stretched ten miles in length through the woods. This in itself was one of the biggest dangers of the plan. A column of men stretched so thin was highly vulnerable if they were discovered by the Union troops at any point along the trail.

Yankee soldiers did notice the sun glinting on the bayonets of Jackson's silent marchers. Hooker had not given orders to attack, but Union Major General Daniel Sickles went ahead and rushed the Confederate rear guard, near Catherine Furnace. Several thousand Yankees came crashing through the underbrush, taking hundreds of surprised Confederates prisoner. The attack was isolated, however, and the rest of Jackson's column continued its long, hot march without interruption.

Confederate soldier on the move

General Hooker, still stationed at Chancellorsville, incorrectly guessed that Sickles had interrupted a full retreat by Lee to the south. Throughout the afternoon, Union scouts rushed to Hooker's headquarters with panicky reports that Jackson was advancing from the left. Hooker and his officers ignored these reports, instead focusing their attention on Lee's troops to the immediate south.

Meanwhile, Stonewall Jackson spent the afternoon quietly deploying his troops into a battle line along a low, wooded ridge about four miles west of Chancellorsville. Jackson's men had tramped a semi-circular route of more than twelve miles through the woods. By 5:00 P.M., masses of Confederate troops extended a mile into the woods on each side of the Turnpike Road, which led directly to the Chancellor House. When the sun dipped low in the sky,

Jackson calmly ordered his troops forward.

The Confederates leaped out of hiding, filling the air with the chilling "Rebel yell," a high-pitched, terrifying screech that Confederate troops employed when they attacked. Surprised Yankees scrambled for cover as thousands of Rebels poured out of the woods. Some Yankees fired their muskets before reeling back in disorder. Union officers screamed hasty commands as Confederate bullets whizzed through the air.

It was near dinnertime in the camps. Union soldier Warren Gloss recalled, "About sundown [many of] the soldiers of the Eleventh Corps, with stacked arms, were boiling their coffee, smoking their pipes, lounging in groups, and playing cards among the baggage wagons . . . all were unprepared, when a few shots were heard . . . and Jackson's men . . . burst upon them like a clap of thunder from a cloudless sky."

The Confederates smashed into the stunned Union troops, sweeping everything before them. The Union line began to collapse like a tumbling row of dominoes. Horses and wagons joined the rush of men crashing through more camps of startled Yankees. Private Luther Mesnard remembered, "To the right or left or in front as far as I could see, everything was fleeing in panic. It seemed to me that the whole army had gone to pieces in a panic."

Along the Union defense line, soldiers managed to get some shots off into the faces of the advancing Rebels but were quickly overrun. The Union's 8th Pennsylvania cavalry regiment bravely galloped into the wave of advancing Rebels, only to lose thirty men and eighty horses within seconds.

The Confederate soldier carrying this book was killed when a bullet ripped through the pages and entered his body.

The attack pushed deeper into the Union lines, moving east toward Chancellorsville. One soldier recalled how the Union rifle volleys and cannonfire

"would mow a road clear through them every time, but they would close up with a yell and come on again."

At Hooker's headquarters at the Chancellor House, Union officer Washington Roebling heard a roaring noise pouring down the Plank Road from the south and west. He then saw his own blue-clad troops running in panicked retreat from the west —"a stampede . . . of yelling, struggling men who had thrown away their muskets, panting for breath, their faces distorted by fear. . . ."

With his entire army in danger of defeat, General Hooker galloped into the mob and tried to organize his panicked troops. He frantically rearranged his remaining men into new defense lines to halt the Rebel charge. When night fell, the Rebel attack slowed. Troops were lost in the dark searching for their regiments through the tangled undergrowth of The Wilderness.

Stonewall Jackson, however, was not satisfied. "Press them!" he still ordered his officers. But there was nothing else his men could do. The Confederate charge had ground to a halt in the impossibly tangled forest.

As his troops settled down for a nervous night in the woods, Jackson and several staff officers left on horseback to scout the enemy position beyond the Confederate lines. A while later, Jackson's group returned toward their troops, trotting through the pitch-dark woods.

As Jackson's party approached the Confederate lines, the men of the 18th North Carolina Regiment stirred in the dark, jittery and confused. All they could hear was horses coming at them. Thinking it was a brigade of Union cavalry, several soldiers shot their muskets at the shadowy figures in the woods.

Out of the darkness, voices shouted, "Cease firing, cease firing! You are firing into your own men!"

In answer, Major John D. Barry yelled out, "Who gave that order? It's a lie! Pour it into them, boys!"

A long row of kneeling Confederates cut loose another fierce musket volley. Their muzzle blasts spit bullets into the scrubby oaks and pines. Wounded horses galloped madly through the woods. Stunned and bloodied soldiers in Confederate uniforms staggered forward and fell. The North Carolina men soon realized their mistake. They had fired on their own Confederate scouting party.

Three bullets had struck Stonewall Jackson in the disastrous gunfire. With the injured Jackson still in the saddle, his horse, "Little Sorrel," galloped wildly through the woods until staff officer Captain R.E. Wilbourn rode up close and grabbed the reins. Wilbourn gently helped Jackson down. With a penknife he slit the left

Confused in the darkness, Confederate soldiers fire on their own commander, Stonewall Jackson.

sleeves of Jackson's raincoat, jacket, and two shirts. He discovered that one musketball had struck Jackson's right hand, another his left forearm. A third had shattered the bone of the general's left arm three inches below the shoulder. He was evacuated to a Confederate field hospital, where a surgeon amputated the arm at the shoulder.

Jeb Stuart

General J.E.B. (Jeb) Stuart took command of Stonewall Jackson's men. Although Jackson's attack had drawn the Confederates within two miles of Chancellorsville, they had not driven far enough. Jackson had wanted to link up with Lee's troops at Catherine Furnace, but the two segments were still divided.

Overnight, General Hooker reorganized his defenses into a tight bulge of lines southwest of Chancellorsville. And more Union troops arrived from the north overnight, bringing their forces to 76,000 men, compared to about 40,000 Confederates.

At 6:00 A.M. on May 3, Jeb Stuart renewed the Rebel attack on Hooker's lines. On a rise of ground called Hazel Grove, Confederate artillerymen fired their cannons into the Union defense lines. Union Captain Charles H. Weygant later described the constant cannon blasts: "The heavens above seemed filled with hot-breathed, shrieking demons."

In the first hours of the day's battle, the Rebels did little more than wear down the Union troops. But by mid-day, the Confederates were advancing on Hooker's lines from all directions, driving them back toward Chancellorsville inch by inch. Hundreds of men fell on both sides. Exploding cannon shells ignited terrific fires in the forest, burning men alive in their tracks.

Meanwhile, Jeb Stuart had risen to the task of

Union soldiers man their cannon post at Chancellorsville. The constant cannonfire of May 3 created havoc for both the Union and Confederate troops.

command. Confederate Major Heros von Borcke recalled that "Stuart was all activity, and wherever the danger was greatest there was he to be found, urging the men forward."

At about 9:30 A.M., General Hooker was standing with his staff on the porch of the Chancellor House. A cannon shell suddenly blasted into a wooden column, which fell and hit Hooker on the head. His officers at first thought he was dead, but he soon rose, dazed and disoriented, his right side paralyzed. Without speaking to his officers, Hooker got on his horse and took off for the rear.

Rebel cannonballs knocked down the chimneys of the Chancellor House, raining bricks on the soldiers below. Exploding shells set the building on fire. Young Sue Chancellor fled with her family from the cellar. She later

With his soldiers cheering, General Lee arrives at the burning Chancellor House; victory was near for the Confederates.

recalled, "The woods around the house were a sheet of fire, the air was filled with shot and shell, horses were running, rearing and screaming, the men a mass of confusion, moaning, cursing and praying."

By mid-morning, the Yankee army was in full retreat toward the Rappahannock River. The Chancellor House was burning furiously when General Lee arrived on horseback at the Chancellorsville crossroads. His soldiers, blackened by the smoke of battle, cheered their victorious leader as he rode past them.

The battle, however, was not yet finished. The Confederates were still vulnerable to General Sedgwick's Union forces at Fredericksburg. Throughout the day, Sedgwick had received confusing orders from the disorganized Union command at Chancellorsville. So Sedgwick finally acted on his own and moved forward. He first fought Jubal Early's unit, and eventually pushed them aside.

When Lee heard that Sedgwick was advancing from his rear, he ordered Lafayette McClaws' division to hurry eastward to join in the defense. These Confederates numbered about 10,000 and delayed Sedgwick's Union advance at Salem Church during the afternoon of May 3 in a bitter, hard afternoon of bloody fighting. The battle continued on May 4, and it appeared that without reinforcements, Sedgwick would not be

John Sedgwick

Hooker's Union troops give up their hold on Chancellorsville and retreat north across the Rappahannock River.

able to break through and reach Chancellorsville.

That night, Hooker (who was recovering from his head wound in a command tent at the rear) gathered his corps commanders and asked them to vote on whether they should continue their retreat or regroup and attack. Through their several days at Chancellorsville, Hooker's men had been eager to fight, and were bitterly disappointed when Hooker failed to give the order to attack. So now they voted in favor of attacking. But for some reason, Hooker ignored their advice and decided that all Union troops, including Sedgwick's, should retreat north across the Rappahannock River.

General Lee later recalled, "Preparations were made to assail [Hooker's] works at daylight on the 6th, but . . . it was found that under cover of the storm and darkness of the night he had retreated over the river." The defeated Yankees slogged through the rain and mud to their old winter camps across the river from Fredericksburg.

Robert E. Lee's triumph at Chancellorsville was one in a series of Confederate victories early in the Civil War.

The horrors of battle: If wounded soldiers were lucky enough to make it to a hospital (right), it was terribly overcrowded. Wounded were often brought to a shade tree (below) near the battlefield, where a doctor would conduct hasty surgery. Both sides suffered tremendous losses of men, animals, and equipment (far right) at Chancellorsville.

   When President Lincoln learned of yet another
Union defeat in Virginia, he exclaimed, "My
God! My God! What will the country say?"
   The South's victory at Chancellorsville was the
bloodiest battle of the war up to that time. The
Yankees suffered 17,278 men killed, wounded,
or missing. The Confederates had suffered 12,764
casualties. Despite his great victory, General Lee
had lost too many men. And he was despondent
that he had lost several of his highest
commanders, especially Stonewall Jackson.

After his arm was amputated, Jackson had been transported to a field hospital, where he developed pneumonia. By May 10, Jackson lay in a deadly fever. His mind in a haze, he died with these last words: "Let us cross over the river and rest under the shade of the trees." All of the South mourned the death of Stonewall Jackson. Many Confederates realized that such a brilliant soldier could not be replaced.

The Civil War struggle continued for two more years on other bloody battlefields. Fresh off the Chancellorsville victory, Lee went on the attack,

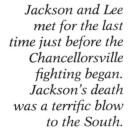

Jackson and Lee met for the last time just before the Chancellorsville fighting began. Jackson's death was a terrific blow to the South.

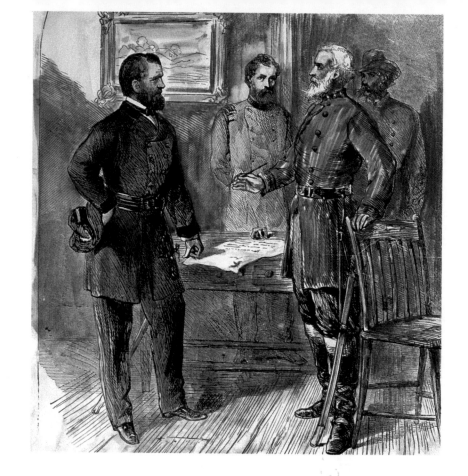

pushing into Maryland and Pennsylvania. But that was as far as he got. Aiming to march on Washington, D.C., Lee was defeated at Gettysburg in July 1863, in a slaughter that cost more than 50,000 casualties for both sides.

Lee then retreated and the war ground into a slow defeat for the South. As Lee's troops and supplies became more depleted, the well-equipped Union army prevailed. On April 9, 1865, Robert E. Lee accepted defeat and surrendered his army to Union General Ulysses S. Grant at Appomattox Court House, Virginia.

INDEX

PHOTO CREDITS

Cover, painting by A. Tholey, National Park Service/from *The Civil War: Rebels Resurgent*, photographed by Larry Sherer, ©1985 Time-Life Books Inc.; 1, painting by Julian Scott. Private collection/Art Resource, NY; 2, Stock Montage, Inc.; 3 (top), Bettmann; 3 (bottom), 4 (both pictures), North Wind Picture Archives; 5 (top), courtesy Robert E. Lee Memorial Association, Stratford Hall Plantation, photographed by Richard Cheek; 5 (bottom), Library of Congress; 6, Stock Montage, Inc.; 7, Bettmann; 9, North Wind Picture Archives; 10, Stock Montage, Inc.; 11 (both pictures), 12, 14, 15, North Wind Picture Archives; 16, painting by Frederick A. Chapman, War Library and Museum, MOLLUS/from *The Civil War: Rebels Resurgent*, photographed by Larry Sherer, ©1985 Time-Life Books Inc.; 17, The Museum of the Confederacy, Richmond, Virginia/from *The Civil War: Rebels Resurgent*, photographed by Larry Sherer, ©1985 Time-Life Books Inc.; 18, Stock Montage, Inc.; 21, Bettmann; 22, Stock Montage, Inc.; 23, from *The Photographic History of the Civil War*, published by The Review of Reviews Company, 1911; 24, 25, Bettmann; 26, 27, North Wind Picture Archives; 28 (both pictures), 29, Bettmann; 30, The Museum of the Confederacy, Richmond, Virginia, photographed by Katherine Wetzel; 31, Stock Montage, Inc.

Picture Identifications:
page 2: Major General John Sedgwick and his staff
page 18: Stonewall Jackson's attack

Project Editors: Shari Joffe and Mark Friedman
Electronic Composition: TJS Design
Original Maps by: TJS Design
Photo Editor: Jan Izzo
Cornerstones of Freedom Logo: David Cunningham

ABOUT THE AUTHOR

Zachary Kent grew up in Little Falls, New Jersey, and received a degree in English from St. Lawrence University. After college, he worked at a New York City literary agency for two years and then launched his writing career. Mr. Kent has had a lifelong interest in American history.